Let's All Listen

Let's All Listen

Songs for Group Work in Settings that Include Students with Learning Difficulties and Autism

Pat Lloyd

Foreword by Adam Ockelford

Jessica Kingsley Publishers
London and Philadelphia

First published in 2008
by Jessica Kingsley Publishers
116 Pentonville Road
London N1 9JB, UK
and
400 Market Street, Suite 400
Philadelphia, PA 19106, USA

www.jkp.com

Copyright © Pat Lloyd 2008
Foreword copyright © Adam Ockelford 2008

The enclosed CD was recorded, edited and produced by Evangelos Himonides, Institute of Education;
Sonustech.com

British Library Cataloguing in Publication Data
A CIP catalogue record for this book is available from the British Library

ISBN 978 1 84310 583 1

Printed and bound in Great Britain by
Printwise (Haverhill) Ltd, Suffolk

Contents

Foreword

There is a growing body of evidence showing that music can play an important role in the education of children with learning difficulties. Its repetitive, regular and therefore predictable structures could have been (and maybe originally were) purpose-made for young minds in the early stages of perceptual and cognitive development – craving order in a complex and confusing world. For teachers, therapists and carers, though, music has much more to offer than pleasing patterns in sound. It can lend its simple, symmetrical shapes to language, reining in the apparently wilful diversity of verbal communication. It can act as an auditory frame of reference for movement – setting the pace for action, and serving as a metaphor for reaching high and stooping low. It can scaffold social encounters, giving children the confidence to embark upon that most risky business of reaching out into the capricious world of other people. Above all, the sheer pleasure of music can permeate any other area of experience and learning which it touches, boosting interest and helping to sustain concentration.

In this book, Pat Lloyd gives practitioners – music specialists and non-specialists alike – the tools to make music work for them in all these ways, as it does for her. She brings to bear her long experience as both music teacher and therapist to achieve that most difficult of tasks: to distil the essence of what she does intuitively, so that others will be able to emulate her approach. Having been privileged to observe Pat in action, I urge you to familiarise yourself with the ideas and materials she sets out in this book, and I heartily commend *Let's All Listen* to you.

Adam Ockelford
Professor of Music, University of Roehampton
September 2007

Acknowledgements

There are a number of people that I would like to thank in relation to the production of this book. Many thanks to:

- Mike Barrie and Suzanne Pennington, Co-headteachers of Heritage House School, and the Governors, for their consistent support and for valuing the development of music at the school so highly.

- The parents at the school, for their enthusiasm for music, and for giving their permission for the use of photographs in the book.

- The staff for their much valued support, energy and commitment.

- Adam Ockelford, Sally Zimmermann and Graham Welch, for their encouragement and help over the years.

- Evangelos Himonides (Sonustech.com) for his expertise and care in recording, editing and producing the CD at the Institute of Education; also Melissa Farnsworth for her singing.

- My family – Andy, Ben and David – for their steadfast support.

- The students with whom I have worked, both currently and in the past. Despite sometimes having to face many adversities, they have shared their love of music with me so generously, and taught me so much.

Part I

Introduction

Introduction

A great deal is now understood about the shared origins of communication and of musical perception in very early human development. It follows that for students who are at the early stages in the development of communication and language, there is particular value in promoting their active expressions of personal and social engagement, using the medium of music which can communicate very directly and powerfully.

The aim of this book is primarily to provide practical ideas and resources for group work, together with a consideration of strategies for adapting musical ideas to meet specific needs. Most of the songs are original; a few are adaptations of traditional folk melodies.

Guidance for use of the songs

The songs were written in response to the needs of students with severe learning difficulties (SLD) or profound and multiple learning difficulties (PMLD), including those who also have autistic spectrum disorders (ASD). Although there may be a wide range of ages of people for whom the songs can be adapted, the term 'student' has been used throughout. For groups that include only students with learning difficulties, the suggested group size is from five to eight, with support staff as appropriate to students' needs. Many of the songs are suitable for mixed ability and for Early Years settings, in which the group size may be larger, according to the needs of the children. Other songs have been successfully used in individual sessions.

When planning a music session it may help to consider the balance between different types of song or activity. A typical session may include:

- An explanation of the content of the session with additional visual support for some students. For example, symbols from the Picture Exchange

Communication System (PECS; Bondy and Frost 1994) or from Writing with Symbols (WWS; Widgit 2000) may be sequenced from left to right on a velcro board. For others it may be more meaningful to use objects of reference to promote their understanding of location and of forthcoming activities.

- A 'Hello song' in which attention is drawn to each individual in turn. Through familiarity with the song the students may be supported in their understanding of place and expected activities.

- At least one song or activity that focuses on listening to one or two students in turn, encouraging exploration of sound-making on different instruments.

- Musical activities in which all participants are making sounds together. This may include work on one of the elements of music, such as dynamics (loud/quiet), pitch (high/low) or tempo (fast/slow).

- Listening to a short piece, played live or using a recording.

- Choice making, either between instruments or between known songs. To allow for choices to be expressed some students may benefit from the use of symbols or photographs with which they have learnt to associate specific songs.

- A song in which everyone is encouraged to make movements in response to music. This may be either in order to make sounds (for example by clapping or stamping) or to move rhythmically with the music. Students' individual responses may be used to lead such songs, with others imitating.

- A 'Goodbye song'. This may be used immediately after a summing up of particular group or individual achievements during the session.

The materials are designed to be used by practitioners from a range of professional backgrounds, including those who are not necessarily confident music specialists. The approach is informed by findings from developmental psychology, and particularly research into parent–infant interactions. The characteristics of the songs and guidance on how they may be used are influenced by a range of research in the field, to which reference is made briefly here. For further background reading, more detail can be found in the 'A brief background to interactive approaches in relation to the use of music' section.

Accompaniments

Chord symbols are suggested for those who may wish to try the songs with simplified harmonies for the accompaniments, using guitar or chromaharp/autoharp. The music is accessible in three different forms.

1. Sample verses may be heard on the CD for each song, and some have additional backing tracks with piano accompaniment only.

2. Simplified chord sequences are suggested for accompaniment of the songs by guitar or chromaharp/autoharp, transposed to a limited range of keys. Guitar chord diagrams and fingering are illustrated on page 21.

3. The vocal line is written with piano accompaniment.

Flexibility

The songs are best if used *flexibly*. In order to reflect the responses of individuals in the group, it may be best to adapt/change the following:

*   Words of the song (using signing/symbols as appropriate).

*   The speed (e.g. different speeds to vary the verses).

*   The dynamics (loudness/quietness).

*   The harmonies of accompaniments.

*   The pitch (how high/low the sounds are).

*   The choice of instruments used.

*   The timing of pauses and use of sound/silence (in anticipation of responses from students).

Using the CD and gaining confidence

For practitioners who are not very confident musically, the CD aims to demonstrate the music so that it can be learnt by ear.

*   It would help to hear the chosen songs a few times in advance of a planned session. The additional backing tracks may also be useful during sessions.

*   Some of us are apprehensive about using our singing voices, but it is important to remember that enthusiasm and sensitivity to the students' needs are far more important than pitching every note in tune!

- For those who are new to the guitar, autoharp or piano, aim for a steady pulse, keeping to the rhythm of the melody as a first step, rather than worrying about the occasional wrong note.

Using repetition

The songs deliberately include much *repetition* (e.g. of melodic phrases, rhythms and bass-line patterns). Research has shown that repetition is an important element of music and of learning (Schaffer 1977; Trehub and Trainor 1998), although it is always a great challenge to avoid the banal!

- There are a variety of keys used, and not only major and minor. The modes of folk music can provide useful alternatives.

- Most of the songs use key words only. Between verses usually only one or two words are changed, allowing maximum opportunity for students to be able to predict and join in with the singing or actions.

- Through repetition students learn to anticipate the next phrase or the ending. Slowing down and also pausing can be introduced to build up a sense of expectation. Students' enjoyment at hearing anticipated sounds can also be enhanced in these ways.

- The songs use a variety of musical styles.

Balancing individual and group attention

The issue of balancing individual and group attention needs to be considered when planning sessions.

- Individual 'turns' in a game need to be kept quite short so that the attention of the group is not lost, and so therefore a verse/chorus structure can be very useful.

- Another device, often suggested in the songs, is to allow pauses within or in between verses so that individuals have the opportunity to initiate an idea which is then used in imitation by the group. The use of carefully timed pauses is an important technique within an interactive approach (Nind and Hewett 1994).

Developing pre-verbal communication skills

Many of the possible objectives that are suggested at the end of each song are concerned with the development of pre-verbal communication skills. For students with ASD it could be the case that these skills may still need to be developed even if the student has some language (Jordan 2005). For example:

- Taking turns (one-to-one or as one of a group).

- The recognition of imitation of one's own sounds.

- The ability to imitate others.

- Experience of 'taking the lead' by initiating sounds/ideas.

- Joint referencing (the ability to recognise that another person has a shared understanding of an activity/event and that the actions of others can be related to one's own).

- Shared attention (the understanding that those in a group are experiencing the same event and the capacity to be attentive to a group activity even when not individually addressed). For students with ASD it is recognised that working as one of a group can be particularly challenging.

- Expressing recognition of 'what's coming next'. The use of pauses during or at the end of a song can build up anticipation and provoke a desire to 'fill in' a pause either with the expected sound/action or with a novel one.

- Understanding the function of communication, and that it can be fun (Frith 1989).

The students' interest in interactions within musical games is of course to be encouraged, and especially any initiation of communication. If appropriate the attention of the group may be drawn to any of the students' initiatives, which may in turn influence the subsequent activity. For example many songs allow for students' actions to lead, with others imitating, as in 'Blues in action' (CD track 33) and 'Follow the leader' (CD track 40). Such techniques may be used to promote the students' understanding of the function and potential power of communication.

The interpretation and development of a student's responses during a session hinges in many respects on the quality of relationships with familiar adults, whether therapists, teachers, parents or support workers. If key workers are present during the session, then ideally they should sit close to the students with whom they work, so that students' responses may be drawn into interactive exchanges. In this way progress in the development of interactions may be more easily generalised beyond the sessions – an important issue particularly for students with ASD for whom generalisation can be problematic (Frith 2003; Jordan 2003).

Creating a shared musical experience

Although many of our aims may be concerned with promoting communication, there remains an entitlement for students to have opportunities to become active participants in shared *musical* experience. Their musical understanding may well develop independently from or exceed other abilities (Ockelford 1996) and so there can be great value in striving to 'tune in' to individuals musically. In this way, it is more likely that their musical abilities will be recognised, acknowledged and celebrated (Ockelford *et al.* 2005). For example, some students with PMLD may need time and vigilance on our part when expressing recognition of, or engagement with, a particular piece or type of music, and perhaps when indicating preferences, in order to ensure that their musical responses are not missed. Also when imitating such students' sound-making, we would normally need to use the same pitch and rhythms, either vocally or on instruments, as it may be that their sensitivity to pitch is well developed. In some of the songs (e.g. 'Whose sound?' (CD track 13)), chords have been suggested for use in two-way musical dialogues, but it would be far preferable to adapt to the pitch and rhythms of individuals' responses.

Using visual supports

Students with ASD are likely to find a number of aspects of group work problematic (Frith 2003). As many of these students may be helped by the use of *visual support* to their understanding, a visual point of focus can be useful within musical games (Prevezer 2002). Therefore props can be used in some songs which may also promote shared attention, for example a parachute, a lycra loop or a sheet which is held on to by students and staff. The success of these games depends on the involvement and enthusiasm of support staff, since at least initially the students may find active involvement to be a challenge.

Involving support staff

Support staff can greatly enhance the sense of shared musical experience by joining in with the singing, playing and actions. This involvement can also serve to model ways of participating for students to copy. Many of the songs and games are reliant on such support; additional volunteers may also provide valuable help.

Working with mixed ability groups

In mixed ability groups the more able students may be challenged in the following ways:

- When they have mastered the main tune, they could perhaps sing a descant line. In songs such as 'Row boat' (CD track 36) they could gain experience of part-singing, and in call/response songs such as 'Follow the leader' (CD track 40) they could sometimes take the lead.

- Instrumental accompaniments could be added, using appropriately pitched instruments. For example, bass chime bars or xylophone could be used to add depth to bass-line patterns, or to contribute extra melodic patterns. Initially a restricted range of notes would be easiest. A number of the songs use simple repeated bass-line patterns in the left-hand piano accompaniment (for example an 'ostinato' or 'drone' bass line could be played by more able students, as in 'Playing on the tambourine' (CD track 20)). Also percussion instruments could be used for songs with repeated rhythmic patterns such as 'What do you eat?' (CD track 14). Students may be encouraged to improvise and explore new patterns of their own.

- Some songs lend themselves to working with partners. More able students could learn to facilitate the involvement of less able students, developing skills in recognising and responding to the needs of others (for example, in CD track 10, 'Let's all find each other's shoulders'). They may also respond to the feel of the music, which is then shared in their interactions with their partner.

Using prompting

Prompting needs to be discussed in advance with support staff, and agreement reached on when and how prompting is to be used with individuals. Generally the use of prompts during sessions needs to be treated with great caution, for the reasons outlined in the next section about the background to interactive approaches. However, for some students, it may be decided that prompting them to sit in a chair during group work is a necessary preliminary step to prepare for an active participation in a shared experience. The most valuable opportunities for students are those that inspire their active involvement in their own learning, allow for the unexpected and promote their own initiatives. Initiative cannot be meaningfully prompted, but it may be that activities that promote initiatives will at first necessitate prompting, in order to set up structures or play routines.

For students with physical difficulties there may be instances in which they benefit from certain sorts of intervention when playing. For example, occasionally support under a wrist may facilitate hand movement for a student. Generally a hand *under* rather than over the student's hand can lead to more control on their part. However, this is an entirely individual matter which is best discussed in advance with the advice of a physiotherapist being sought if necessary.

If a student (for example, one with PMLD) is unable to make a rewarding sound on a particular instrument without prompts then, instead, Soundbeam (www.soundbeam.co.uk) and switches can offer many potentially motivating alternatives (for example, in CD track 1, 'Let's all listen'). When movements which are familiar to the student are used, there are ample opportunities for active musical involvement without a dependency on prompts – and therefore a much richer and more meaningful involvement is achieved.

Recording students' responses to measure progress

The recording of students' responses is of great importance as a means of measuring progress over time towards intended learning outcomes. In order to achieve this, either individual or group recording sheets need to be filled in after sessions, or during sessions if possible.

Using songs to express moods and emotions

Music is particularly powerful for expressing *moods and emotions*. On many levels there is much to be gained by supporting the development of students' recognition and understanding of emotions – both their own and others. This may well be a particularly significant need of students with ASD (Frith 2003). Although work on the understanding of emotion commonly features in schools' curricula, and its importance recognised, it is often seen as difficult to teach and so music may be particularly valuable in helping to support such understanding. Students' appreciation of the expressive qualities of music may also be enhanced by focusing on what music might be 'saying' to them.

One song (CD track 43, 'Sad and happy') is specifically about moods. However, other songs could also be used to highlight a range of emotions. For example, the feeling of excitement could be discussed in 'Going out!' (CD track 5) for students who like school trips; or a student's expression of mood within games can be commented on during the song, perhaps drawing the attention of others to the expression of, for example, excitement in their face. A mirror could also be used to help an individual to see expressions in his or her own face. The use of symbols and photographs has also been helpful in supporting such understanding.

Building on passive or incidental behaviours

The songs aim to use simple ideas, with much repetition, so that there are plenty of opportunities for students to express recognition and familiarity. Through their anticipation within familiar routines it is to be hoped that the initiation of active involvement will develop. However, to begin with their *passive or incidental movements* may well be useful starting points – through others' imitation of these movements, a student may begin to learn the power (and fun!) of being in a leading role. For example, the focus of each verse in 'Blues in action' (CD track 33) can use any movement or sounds made by a member of the group, whether this is intentional or not. The music itself may well evoke responses leading to an action to be shared in the next verse.

Using signs, symbols and objects of reference

The language used within songs is also very simple, using key-words and much repetition of short phrases. Not only is the aim to foster familiarity, but this simplicity also allows for plenty of opportunities for using *signs, symbols and objects of reference*; for example, Makaton (Walker and Armfield 1982), a simplified version of British Sign Language, and symbols such as PECS (Bondy and Frost 1994), Boardmaker (Mayer-Johnson 2004) or WWS (Widgit 2000). The focus of verses in some songs, such as 'What do you eat?' (CD track 14), may be chosen by an individual using signs or symbols. Initially a restricted range of symbols may be made available, depending on the abilities of the individual. This may be differentiated for more able symbol-users to include a much wider range (perhaps including discrimination from some irrelevant symbols, and eventually a PECS book). Symbols can be devised to represent different songs (or pieces of recorded music), so that choices can be made, as expressions of musical preference. For a student with autism this may well be more successful than relying on signing or speaking, since the symbols offer a more concrete visual representation which can be scanned and considered before a decision is made (Bondy and Frost 1994).

Notes on the accompaniments and the CD

Accompaniments

Almost all the songs include a suggested piano accompaniment, and most are also provided with simplified accompaniments which use a range of only seven chords. A chromaharp/autoharp or a guitar could be used to provide additional harmonic and rhythmic support to the singing.

Guitar chords

Major chords

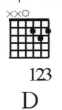

123

D

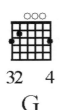

32 4

G

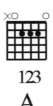

123

A

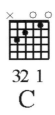

32 1

C

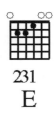

231

E

Minor chords

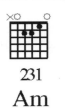

231

Am

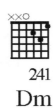

241

Dm

× = silent string, ○ = open string

The CD

The CD contains sample recordings of all the songs, so that they can be picked up by ear. For most songs two verses have been recorded to demonstrate the songs; CD track numbers correspond to the song numbers.

A final word

All of these songs developed from work with individuals or groups of students, to whom I am indebted. For practitioners who are new to this style of work, the use of adapted well-known songs and tunes is an excellent starting point when devising new activities for your own settings. I am in no doubt that with this approach, and from whatever professional background, or starting point, exciting new songs will develop from practice based on meeting the needs of the students. Flexibly adapting shared musical activity to meet individual needs can indeed be valuable, successful and rewarding, in so very many different ways.

A brief background to interactive approaches in relation to the use of music

The above guidance for the use of songs reflects an interactive approach, informed by the growing body of research into early parent–infant interactions. 'Intensive interaction' techniques have been developed by Nind and Hewett (1994) in the light of such research, and these will be discussed in this chapter. Some of the research into infants' development of communication has also highlighted the importance of musical elements in parent–infant dialogues. A number of techniques have since developed in which music has a central place in the promotion of interactive play between practitioners and developmentally young students. Interactive approaches to music-making share the aim of making use of the unique power of music as a fundamental mode of communication.

> Music is our oldest form of expression, older than language or art; it begins with the voice, and with our overwhelming need to reach out to others. In fact, music is man far more than words, for words are abstract symbols which convey factual meaning. Music touches our feelings more deeply than most words and makes us respond with our whole being... We need music, I believe, as much as we need each other. (Menuhin and Davis 1979, p.1)

The quality of music as being an essential part of human experience is discussed by writers and researchers spanning a wide area of thinking (Papousek 1996; Small 1999; Storr 1997; Trevarthen 1999). In the quotation above, Yehudi Menuhin refers to these essential qualities, which make music relevant to us all:

- Responsiveness to music begins at the very earliest stages of life, and in many ways is more elemental than language.

- The voice is often an initial shared medium of both music and language.

- It is part of our need and desire to communicate.

- It communicates feelings and emotions in a unique and particularly direct way.

- It can create, and be an expression of, experience which may be both intensely personal and yet also shared.

There is evidence of these qualities in so many features of past and present cultures. Archaeologist and historian Steven Mithen (2005) refers to evidence of the central place of music from the very earliest of times in the development of human communication and social organisation. There is also evidence from developmental psychology over the past twenty years that points to the great importance of musical responsiveness in early infancy. For example, Trevarthen (1999) suggests that musical elements of early parent–infant interaction are an integral part of the development of communication skills. Papousek (1996) and Trehub and Trainor (1998) also refer to the musical qualities of parent–infant interactions, such as the use of exaggerated pitch differences in the use of speech when directed at a baby. Such pitch differences heighten the melodic contours of speech, leading to a 'sing-song' quality in the use of the voice. It has also been shown that the use of repeated rhythmic patterns and phrases, changes in speed and the use of expectant pauses to build up anticipation are all significant elements in the development of pre-verbal communication skills. Research into the development of musical perception affirms our predisposition to musical responsiveness, which is evident even prior to birth (Welch 2005).

Welch (2006) also discusses the particular significance of song during child development, including the earliest stages of infancy. He refers to vocal sound as 'one of the defining features of humanity' (2005, p.239) with a significant overlap between its two main manifestations, singing and speech. For a young infant, singing and speech are discussed as being inextricably linked since both are potentially perceived as meaningful and communicative, using the shared medium of vocal sound. Trehub and Trainor (1998) also refer to the developmental and cultural significance of play songs, used extensively in early childhood across different cultures.

Intensive interaction

Research into parent–infant interaction has informed the work of Melanie Nind and Dave Hewett (1994), which has since been influential in special education. They have developed 'intensive interaction' techniques in which the aim is to develop pre-verbal communication skills in children with SLD and PMLD and also with those who are on the autistic spectrum. Intensive interaction makes use of the range of interactive games which normally occur during parent–infant interactions. The emphasis is initially on promoting the student's enjoyment of individual attention from a familiar adult, with mutual focusing on each other's sounds or facial expressions. The intention is that over time sequences of interactions become more elaborate, to include turn-taking, anticipation within play sequences, repetition, and imitation. There is a great emphasis on the need for sensitively 'tuning in' to the interests and attention of the student and the use of expectant pauses within familiar play routines. Such pauses are used to empower the student to express recognition and anticipation within interactions, and also to allow opportunities to communicate their own initiatives, whether this be a sound, action or facial expression. The approach highlights the role of the learner as an active partner: interactions are led and maintained by the student.

Research into parent–infant interactions and the work of Nind and Hewett (1994) have in turn informed the development of interactive styles of work when using music in individual and group sessions. At Sunderland House in Nottingham for pupils with ASD, the techniques of 'musical interaction therapy' have been developed over some time, as described by Wendy Prevezer (2002), a speech and language therapist who is also a musician. Individual children are accompanied in their sessions by a familiar adult, who could be a key worker or parent. A second adult provides a flexible musical framework, by using familiar songs and play routines within which interactions between the child and the key worker may be supported. Songs often use traditional tunes, with words adapted for a particular game. As in intensive interaction, techniques such as the use of expectant pauses within songs are used extensively, allowing the child to lead interactions. The approach has been evaluated by Wimpory, Chadwick and Nash (1995) and Chandler *et al.* (2002) who found that there was successful fostering of joint attention and understanding and that the benefits generalised beyond therapy. Prevezer (2002) has also developed inventive and effective techniques for group work, using the same principles for promoting shared attention, motivation for communication and the development of pre-verbal communication skills.

Similarly the work of Margaret Corke (2002) very imaginatively makes use of interactive styles of work in group work using music. The Soundabout organisation has also developed techniques using resonance boards to promote shared attention and sound-making in groups. In common with all interactive approaches there is great emphasis placed on the child's responses and initiatives, using these to lead interchanges, the importance of which is amply supported by research, as cited by Nind and Hewett (1994). Such initiatives are promoted within familiar play routines which build on the child's anticipation of what might follow. The use of carefully timed pauses is also considered to be crucial to these approaches, allowing time and frequent opportunities for the student's expectations or new ideas to be expressed, acknowledged and responded to. For example, the silence of a sudden pause during a familiar game or routine may be highly empowering for a child who rarely has the opportunity to take a leading role in pre-verbal dialogues. By initiating a sound to break the silence, he or she is thus allowed to assume that position of importance and control.

Imitation and repetition have also been shown to be highly significant features of learning through interaction (Schaffer 1977). Direct imitation is highlighted as a means of 'reflecting back' the child's sound-making or actions, and allowing him or her to take a leading role in the dialogue. However, the use of slight variations between repetitions is also shown to have value in promoting explorations of different sounds or behaviours, whilst the adult needs to remain cautious about taking on a role which becomes dominant. The child's initiatives are considered of paramount importance in promoting his or her need and desire to communicate (as also confirmed by research; see, for example, Bruner 1983). Therefore the use of prompting also needs to be considered with great caution, as discussed by Margaret Corke (2002). After all, when a child initiates a communicative behaviour this derives from the desire to do so, which cannot be prompted in any meaningful way. Rather, our role as staff is to promote the desire to initiate communication through showing that it can be empowering and enjoyable and has real intrinsic value. The great fun which may be shared within musical games with developmentally young children is evidence of the special place that music has in this respect (Trehub and Trainor 1998).

Music therapy

Music therapists have long been engaged in exploiting the unique power of music to promote communication, often using improvised music as a medium within musical dialogue. Music therapy gradually developed in Britain during the 1960s, and, like other arts therapies, it is now a state registered profession, for which qualification requires one or two years of postgraduate study. Although music therapy has a separate history and identity from intensive interaction and related musically interactive styles of work, there is a shared emphasis on allowing the child's initiatives to lead. Flexibility is seen as crucial in accommodating, acknowledging and reflecting upon the nature of a child's expressions of musical responsiveness. Musical improvisation is therefore regarded as an ideal medium within which reciprocal dialogues may be explored and developed (Bunt 1994). During its forty-year history there has been a steady growth in research upon which to base practice (Wigram, Pedersen and Bonde 2002).

Music therapists work within a wide range of different fields, and also use a number of different approaches (Bunt and Hoskyns 2002). Amongst therapists who work in educational settings for children with special needs, there are those who use an approach that is specifically based on the findings of developmental psychology. For these therapists there is acknowledgement of the particular relevance of research into parent–infant interaction, especially when working with children with very restricted communication and language (Lloyd 2003). There is also recognition that the influence of a developmental approach is shared between a number of professions, including speech and language therapy and teaching; valuable collaborative work may be facilitated through this common influence and shared paradigm (Lloyd 2003; Warriner and Bridges 2006).

Music therapy literature does acknowledge an overlap between teaching and therapy in special education (Robertson 2000). Some therapists refer to this as a 'grey area' (Wigram *et al.* 2002, p.34; Bunt 2003, p.191) in which therapy and teaching are far from distinctly separate. It is beyond the scope of this short background to enter into the therapy/education debate, which is discussed elsewhere by a number of authors (Bunt 2003; Ockelford 2000; Robertson 2000; Wigram *et al.* 2002). However, it is interesting to compare the situation with developments in the field of autism. Rita Jordan, a leading authority on autism, highlights the need for 'a therapeutic approach to education, and an educational approach to therapy' (Jordan 2003, p.8; also discussed in Jordan 2005). She considers that there is much to be gained by viewing therapy and education as part of a continuum rather than as separate approaches – a concept that is also discussed by Wigram *et al.* (2002) and Robertson (2000). With reference to the range of interventions now available in the field of autism, Jordan advocates an eclectic way of working, based on an individualised approach to meeting needs (Jordan 2005). She believes that it is these needs that should drive our choices about practice. Consequently methods should be adapted to suit the individual, rather than the child being required to adapt to any specific method. With an eclectic approach, one method may be used alongside another, as appropriate to each child. Our perceptions of how students' needs may be identified and met are continually evolving in the light of increasing knowledge and research; the enormous changes within special education in the last few decades are evidence of this. In turn professional adaptability must therefore be seen as a necessity, along with an ongoing commitment to a collaborative approach towards meeting needs, the value of which is recognised from both educationalists' and therapists' perspectives (for example, Jellison 2006; Lacey 1998; Oldfield 2006; Warwick 1995). Above all, I would argue that these areas of overlap between therapy and education should be regarded as fertile ground for continuing to develop creative methods and approaches of common interest, in the quest to meet individual need, and to the advantage of future practice and provision.

For any practitioners or parents who are engaged in using music with people with severe communication problems, there is indeed much to be gained by applying a knowledge of the role of musical elements and perception in early infancy. An individualised approach to meeting needs calls for a considered view of the available range of methods, an innovative and flexible style of work and a commitment to work collaboratively with a range of professionals and with parents. Research into the efficacy of different approaches is of great value and with the benefit of such research there is now a greater range of evidence on which to base practice. The ongoing drive towards evidence-based practice is likely to affect practitioners from a range of backgrounds. As ever, the need for further research in this important area therefore continues to be a priority.

References

Bondy, A.S. and Frost, L.A. (1994) 'The Delaware Autistic Program.' In S.L. Harris and J.S. Handleman (eds) *Preschool Education Programs for Children with Autism.* Austin: Pro-Ed.

Bruner, J. (1983) *Child's Talk: Learning to Use Language.* Oxford: Oxford University Press.

Bunt, L. (1994) *Music Therapy: An Art beyond Words.* London: Routledge.

Bunt, L. (2003) 'Music therapy with children: A complementary service to music education?' *British Journal of Music Education 20,* 2, 179–195.

Bunt, L. and Hoskyns, S. (eds) (2002) *The Handbook of Music Therapy.* Hove: Brunner-Routledge.

Chandler, S., Christie, P., Newson, E. and Prevezer, W. (2002) 'Developing a diagnostic and intervention package for 2 to 3 year olds with autism.' *Autism: The International Journal of Research and Practice 7,* 1, 47–69.

Corke, M. (2002) *Approaches to Music through Communication*. London: Fulton.

Frith, U. (1989) 'A new look at language and communication in autism.' *British Journal of Disorders of Communication 24*, 123–140.

Frith, U. (2003) *Autism: Explaining the Enigma* (2nd edn). Oxford: Blackwell.

Jellison, J.A. (2006) 'Including Everyone.' In G.E. McPherson (ed.) *The Child as Musician*. Oxford: Oxford University Press.

Jordan, R. (2003) *Historical Overview of Interventions*. Module 3, Unit 2, Section 3, Web-Based University Certificate of Education (ASDs). School of Education, University of Birmingham (unpublished).

Jordan, R. (2005) 'Autistic Spectrum Disorders.' In A. Lewis and B. Norwich (eds) *Special Teaching for Special Children? Pedagogies for Inclusion*. Maidenhead: Open University Press.

Lacey, P. (1998) 'Multidisciplinary Teamwork.' In C. Tilstone, L. Florian and R. Rose (eds) *Promoting Inclusive Practice*. London: Routledge.

Lloyd, P. (2003) *An Evaluation of the Educational Benefits of Music Therapy for Students with SLD, with Particular Reference to the Development of Communication and Language*. Unpublished MEd dissertation. School of Education, University of Birmingham.

Mayer-Johnson (2004) *Boardmaker*. Solana Beach, CA. Accessed on 3/3/07 at www.mayer-johnson.com.

Menuhin, Y. and Davis, C.W. (1979) *The Music of Man*. London: MacDonald and Jane's.

Mithen, S. (2005) *The Singing Neanderthals: The Origin of Music, Language, Mind and Body*. London: Phoenix.

Nind, M. and Hewett, D. (1994) *Access to Communication: Developing the Basics of Communication with People with Severe Learning Difficulties through Intensive Interaction*. London: Fulton.

Ockelford, A. (1996) *All Join In! A Framework for Making Music with Children and Young People Who Are Visually Impaired and Have Learning Disabilities*. London: Royal National Institute for the Blind.

Ockelford, A. (2000) 'Music in the education of children with severe or profound learning difficulties: Issues in U.K. provision, a new conceptual framework, and proposals for research.' *Psychology of Music 28*, 197–217.

Ockelford, A., Welch, G., Zimmermann, S. and Himonides, E. (2005) 'Mapping musical development in children with PMLD: The Sounds of Intent Project.' *The SLD Experience 43*, 20–23.

Oldfield, A. (2006) *Interactive Music Therapy – A Positive Approach*. London: Jessica Kingsley Publishers.

Papousek, M. (1996) 'Intuitive Parenting: A Hidden Source of Musical Stimulation in Infancy.' In I. Deliege and J. Sloboda (eds) *Musical Beginnings*. Oxford: Oxford University Press.

Prevezer, W. (2002) *Entering into Interaction* (3rd edn). Unpublished: available from The Elizabeth Newson Centre, 272 Longdale Lane, Ravenshead, Nottingham NG15 9AH.

Robertson, J. (2000) 'An educational model for music therapy: The case for a continuum.' *British Journal of Music Therapy 14*, 1, 41–46.

Schaffer, H.R. (ed.) (1977) *Studies in Mother-Infant Interaction*. London: Academic Press.

Small, C. (1999) 'Musicking – The meanings of performing and listening. A lecture.' *Music Education Research 1*, 1, 9–21.

Soundabout. Accessed on 20/2/06 at www.soundabout.org.uk.

Storr, A. (1997) *Music and the Mind*. London: HarperCollins.

Trehub, S. and Trainor, L. (1998) 'Singing to infants: Lullabies and play songs.' *Advances in Infant Research 12*, 43–77.

Trevarthen, C. (1999) 'Musicality and the intrinsic motive pulse: Evidence from human psychobiology and infant communication.' *Musicae Scientiae* Special Issue 1999–2000, 155–215.

Walker, M. and Armfield, A. (1982) 'What is the makaton vocabulary?' *Special Education: Forward Trends 8*, 3, 19–20.

Warriner, I. and Bridges, C. (2006) 'Combining speech and language therapy and music therapy.' *The Royal College of Speech and Language Therapy November Bulletin 655*, 14–15.

Warwick, A. (1995) 'Music Therapy in the Education Service: Research with Autistic Children and Their Mothers.' In T. Wigram (ed.) *The Art and Science of Music Therapy*. Chur, Switzerland: Harwood Academic Publishers.

Welch, G. (2005) 'Singing as Communication.' In D. Miell, R. MacDonald and D.J. Hargreaves (eds) *Music as Communication*. New York: Oxford University Press.

Welch, G. (2006) 'Singing and Vocal Development.' In G.E. McPherson (ed.) *The Child as Musician*. Oxford: Oxford University Press.

Widgit (2000) *Writing with Symbols*. Accessed on 31/7/07 at www.widgit.com.

Wigram, T., Pedersen, I.N. and Bonde, L.O. (2002) *A Comprehensive Guide to Music Therapy: Theory, Clinical Practice, Research and Training*. London: Jessica Kingsley Publishers.

Wimpory, D., Chadwick, P. and Nash, S. (1995) 'Brief report: Musical interaction therapy for children with autism. An evaluative case study with two year follow-up.' *Journal of Autism and Developmental Disorders 25*, 5, 541–552.

Part II

Songs and Activities

Let's all listen

CD track 1

Pat Lloyd

Quietly and expectantly

Let's all li - sten, let's all li - sten,

ppp

With pedal throughout

let's all li - sten to Sa - ski - a play - ing the harp.
Myles

*Ad lib while pupil plays,
continuing the bass line*

Activities

This can be used with a cimbale (harp-like instrument) pre-tuned to play an appropriate range of notes (e.g. an octave of notes up from G which correspond to the white notes on a keyboard). Similarly a guitar or other tuned string instruments can be used. Alternatively Soundbeam could be used on a harp setting.

The pupil plays after each verse is sung to them, and their explorations can be supported by the accompaniment.

Possible objectives

- Experience of producing and exploring sounds on strings or using Soundbeam.

- Waiting until the end of the singing before playing, i.e. waiting for a musical cue.

- Hearing and producing sounds that are quiet.

- Taking turns as one of a group.

Guitar version

Rather than using chords, this may be best using two notes (G) played an octave apart.

School song

CD track 2

Words written by different classes in the school;
music by Pat Lloyd

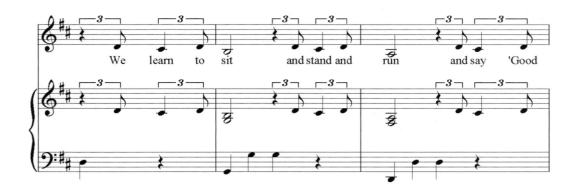

We learn to sit and stand and run and say 'Good

morn-ing' to ever- y - one. We learn to sit and stand and

Return to chorus

run, That's why we go to school. We go to

Activities

This can be developed to include verses from each class, reflecting activities within that class. These are the verses written by Heritage House School's classes:

For a TEACCH class or department:

We do our tasks, we use our PECS.
We go for walks every day.
We do our tasks, we use our PECS.
That's why we go to school.

For an older class:

We do our ASDAN, we run a shop.
We swim at Chesham, we shop and cook...

Or more general verses could be used; for example:

We learn to swim, we learn to play,
And we're with friends every day...

The chorus can be adapted to fit with the name of the school.

The song lends itself to the use of signing/symbols, using a restricted number of words and much repetition. It can be used at most whole-school events, marking these as shared social experiences.

Guitar version

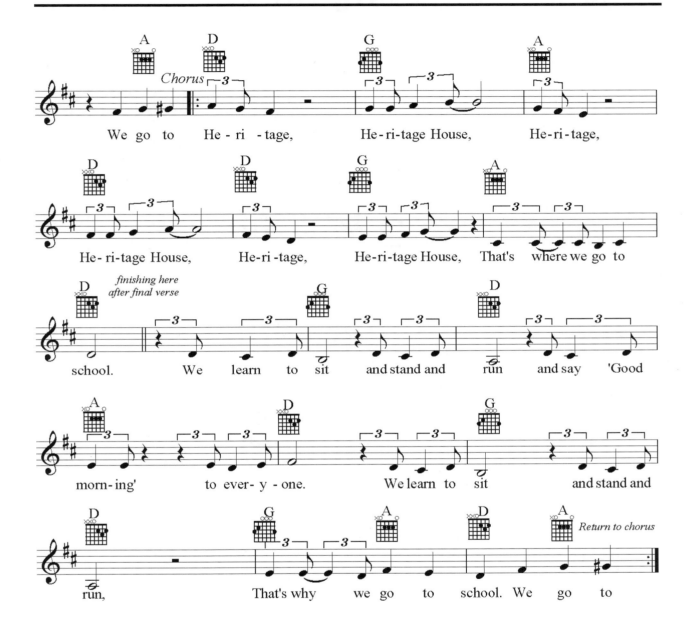

Who is next taking turns?

CD track 3

Activities

Taking turns in imitation of another person – either the student or the adult takes the lead, depending on the individual student. Initially perhaps just one sound only is used, and then working towards patterns of two, etc.

Alternatively, some students may work on imitation of a hitting v. scratching sound, or hitting v. shaking.

At first the adult and student could share the same instrument, moving on towards having one each.

Possible objectives

- To recognise imitation of short patterns.

- To be able to imitate a method of sound-making (hitting/scratching).

- To be able to imitate one sound, when contrasted with 'lots and lots' of sounds.

- To be able to imitate one/two/three sounds as appropriate to the individual.

- To imitate loud/quiet and high/low.

Guitar version

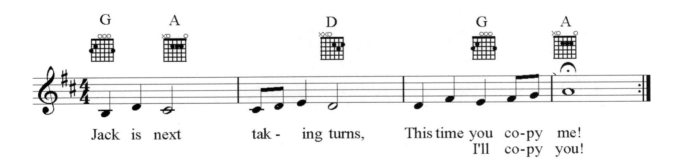

Jack is next   tak - ing turns,   This time you co-py me!
                                                  I'll co-py you!

Where is Chloe?

CD track 4

Activities

One pupil 'hides' – under a large scarf, or behind the piano, etc. At the pause, he or she is prompted to show his or her face by pulling away the scarf, or jumping out of the hiding place. The song then continues with words as appropriate (e.g. 'here she is, hiding behind the chair').

Possible objectives

- To link an event (pulling off the scarf) with a particular point in the music.

- Learning to anticipate 'what comes next'.

- To have control over the resumption of others' singing.

- To promote social awareness/learning names of others and focusing on each in turn.

Guitar version

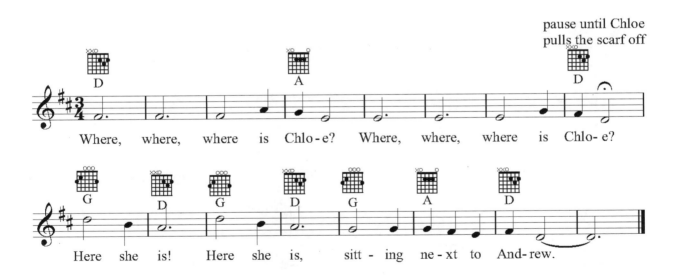

Going out!

CD track 5

Pat Lloyd

Activities

Sing 'Going out on a walk to the town' or change according to the situation (e.g. 'Going out on a big red bus').

At the end of the song a sound is made as appropriate to the trip (traffic sounds, rain, people talking, helicopter, sounds of a shop till). A switch can activate sounds using a CD of sound effects, or the switchbox from Soundbeam. A pupil could be 'in charge' of the switches. Another pupil indicates what they can hear using objects of reference, symbols or photographs.

For a trip (real or imagined) to a farm, animal noises could be used (available on sound-effects CDs).

Possible objectives

- Identifying sounds, matching sound to symbols or photographs.

- Waiting for the end of a song before activating a switch.

- To promote imaginative play using sound/music.

- Additional dramatic elements could be introduced, e.g. arranging chairs to make a 'bus'.

Guitar version

43

Listen!

CD track 6

Pat Lloyd

Activities

One student hides behind a screen and produces a sound using one of a restricted range of instruments (e.g. drum, block, bells). Another student (or the group) is asked to 'say' which instrument is being played (e.g. pointing to/finding a matching instrument, symbol or photograph). On finding a matching instrument the student then plays (with part 2).

Possible objectives

- Sound-matching.

- Identifying different sounds with corresponding sound-makers.

- Understanding the concept of 'same'/'different'.

- Learning 'names'/'labels' for instruments by touch, tactile or visual symbols, photographs, speech.

- Sound-making with another person.

Guitar version

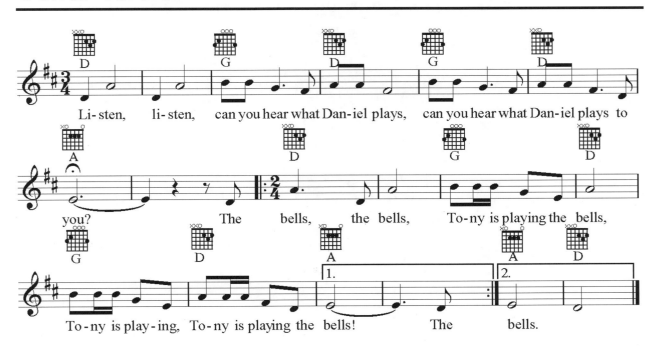

Five big elephants

CD track 7

Pat Lloyd

Activities

Either there is a shared focus of five elephant puppets or this could be individualised so that pupils start with five each. At the end of each verse the pupils take one away and the elephants are re-counted. At first there is no accompaniment to the last verse ('No big elephants, all gone away'), until the bass chimes again describe the sound of the returning elephants, getting louder and faster as they approach.

The accompaniment here is simply two bass chime bars which produce a low, rich, resonant sound. These are played slowly for the first five verses, emulating the sounds of the elephants' feet.

Perhaps one or two pupils could provide the sounds on the bass chime bars or on Boomwhackers.

Possible objectives

- Reinforcement of number concepts up to five (or just on the concept of one).
- Working on the anticipation of repetition, followed by the changes at the end.
- Working on awareness of tempi: fast/slow. Also dynamics: loud/quiet.
- Playing slow/fast with the song.
- An understanding that sounds and music can tell stories.

Taking turns with me

CD track 8

Pat Lloyd

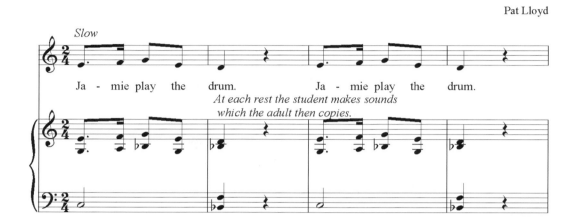

Ja - mie play the drum. Ja - mie play the drum.

*At each rest the student makes sounds
which the adult then copies.*

Tak - ing turns with me Tak - ing turns with me.

Activities

The aim of the song is to hold the attention of the group while allowing for individuals to take turns at sound-making.

Each student takes turns with the adult who is playing the piano, guitar or a shared instrument. This could be any form of sound (including vocal sound or sound activated by a switch). Alternatively, it could be used to work on the concept of 'one' sounds.

Initially the student could lead for the adult to copy. The song could also be developed to include the student imitating the adult.

Possible objectives

- Waiting for a musical cue before producing sound.

- Turn-taking.

- Working on the concept of 'one' sound.

- Reinforcing the concept of 'same'.

Guitar version

Taking turns (for two students)

CD track 9

Pat Lloyd

Activities

The song acts as a recurring chorus, designed to hold the attention of the students even when it may not be their turn to play. At the end of each chorus, two students are invited to take turns with each other using either one shared instrument, or one of a matching pair of instruments, or two contrasting instruments or switches. The intention is to promote opportunities for them to explore how to develop a 'conversation' in sound.

Initially it may be appropriate to have one student taking turns with a member of staff.

Possible objectives

- To learn, or to generalise, turn-taking skills.

- To use patterns of sound in a musical 'conversation'.

- To focus on each other.

- To develop skills that may promote reciprocal play.

Guitar version

Tak-ing turns,   tak-ing turns,   Let's li-sten to Luke and Na-ta-sha.

Tak-ing turns,   tak-ing turns,   Let's li-sten to Luke and Na-ta-sha.

Let's all find each other's shoulders

CD track 10

Pat Lloyd

Let's all find each

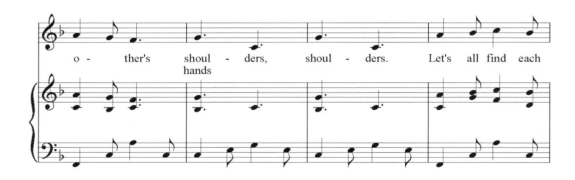

o - ther's shoul - ders, shoul - ders. Let's all find each

o - ther's shoul - ders just like this.

Activities

There are two main options:

1. Students face their partner. Working in pairs they find each other's shoulders, heads, arms, legs, etc. They may be encouraged to sway with the beat.

2. The group sits on chairs in a circle and focuses on each individual in turn, watching out for their initiatives and movements, e.g.

   Let's all find Dawn's hand, Dawn, Dawn.
   Let's all find Dawn's hand just like this.

   A member of staff strokes the individual's hand or moves with the music, while being attentive to the student's wishes and preferences.

   Different students may have different verses: head, arm, leg, etc.

   In a mixed ability group, a more able pupil may take the place of a member of staff, learning to 'read' the expressions and preferences of a pupil with PMLD and to respect his or her needs.

Possible objectives

- Focusing on each other in co-operative play and watching each other's responses.

- Experiencing movement with music and anticipating when it may be one's own turn.

- Finding a named student and finding a specified part of their body, e.g. head, hand and arm.

Guitar version

Let's all find each o - ther's shoul - ders, shoul - ders.
hands

Let's all find each o - ther's shoul - ders just like this.

One monkey jumps up!

CD track 11

Activities

The group holds out the edge of a large piece of lycra. A number of students have a monkey puppet/toy under their chair. At the start of each verse one monkey is thrown into the centre of the lycra and staff/pupils make it 'jump' by lifting up the lycra. Then 'two monkeys jump up... three... four... five', finishing with the chanting 'ready, steady, go' and making all the monkeys jump off.

The reggae setting on a keyboard/clavinova fits well with the song.

Possible objectives

- Shared attention and involvement.
- Linking song with events.
- Promoting imaginative play.
- Number concepts 'one' or 'one to five' as appropriate. Also 'none'/'all gone'.
- The concept of 'up'.

Guitar version

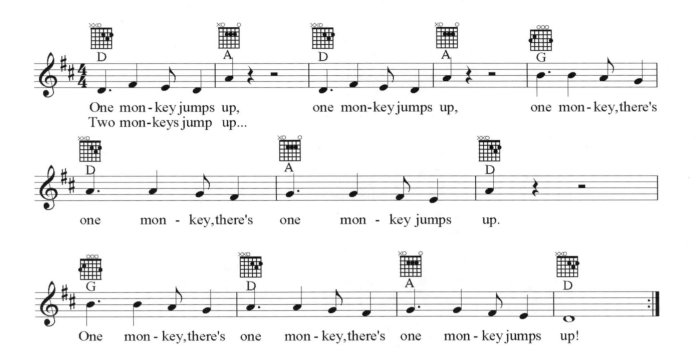

One mon-key jumps up, one mon-key jumps up, one mon-key, there's
Two mon-keys jump up...

one mon - key, there's one mon - key jumps up.

One mon - key, there's one mon - key, there's one mon - key jumps up!

Make him jump up and down!

CD track 12

Swedish folk tune,
adapted by Pat Lloyd

Make him jump up and down, Make him jump up and down _(repeat)_____

_____ Make him jump up and down then jump to Tom.
...Sam.

Activities

Another game with the shared visual focus of a large piece of lycra which the students are prompted to hold at the edges. A soft toy is thrown into the middle (maybe a frog, or a grasshopper puppet/toy) and made to jump up with the corresponding words of the song. At the end of each verse the toy is encouraged to jump to a different person in the group, who is named at the end of the song. The next verse resumes when the child throws the toy back onto the lycra.

Possible objectives

- To allow opportunities to develop shared attention in a group setting.

- To steer the focus of the group towards its individual members.

- To develop a sense of shared enjoyment in group work, heightened by a sense of anticipation which builds up with familiarity with the musical game.

Guitar version

Make him jump up and down, Make him jump up and down   *(repeat)*

Make him jump up and down then jump to Tom.

Whose sound?

CD track 13

Pat Lloyd

Activities

This is designed for a group that includes students with PMLD. For a student who is already in a vocal mood, the song can be addressed to him or her, with pauses included so that the group are listening out for sounds. (Whenever sounds are made, the best response may be to jump straight to the second section – 'She goes…')

The student's sounds may then be imitated to encourage further sound-making. It would be best to match the pitch of the vocalisation if possible, vocally and/or on the accompanying instrument. This works best if approached very flexibly, and may possibly lead to a dialogue of taking turns in sound-making.

If a student is not interested in vocalising, then instruments, switches or Soundbeam could be used in similar ways.

Possible objectives

- To have experience of one's own sounds being imitated.

- To recognise such imitation.

- To take an active part in a shared musical experience.

- To listen to the sounds of other students.

Guitar version

Chords are suggested on the version for piano accompaniment, although it would be best to adapt to the sounds made by the student.

What do you eat?

CD track 14

Pat Lloyd

Tho-mas likes his food. What does he eat? Tho-mas likes his food.

What does he eat? He likes cheese bur-ger, That's what he eats,

pause to point to/ sign another favourite food

He likes cheese bur-ger, That's what he eats!

Activities

Using signing, or a range of symbols, each student is invited to say which are their favourite foods (often a very motivating topic!). A large shared velcro board could be used with A4-sized symbols. The number of symbols would need to be appropriate to each student. For PECS book users preferences could be stated in their usual way.

Possible objectives

- To generalise the use of signs or symbols to a different setting.

- To express preference and to hear the song reflect this.

- To understand that the preferences of others may differ from one's own.

- (For more able students) To improvise rhythmic patterns based on a set beat.

Alternative accompaniments

The left-hand part of the piano could be used with the vocal line, or this rhythm could be played on a drum by a student or member of staff.

Two by two

CD track 15

Pat Lloyd

looked just the same. They made friends, and then there were

two! An two!

Activities

There are different possibilities with this song. Both suggestions rely on the use of a pause in between verses.

1. Animal toys or puppets could be given to some or all members of the group – a range of animals, including two of each. In each verse a pupil is encouraged to look around the group to find an animal which is the same as theirs. At the end of each verse all check to see if there are two of the same animal together. Others have turns until all of the animals are in pairs.

2. A large velcro board is used with A4-sized symbols showing a range of animals. (The group leader has a second set of animal symbols.) In turn students are given a symbol by the group leader and during each verse they are encouraged to look at the board to find one which is the same.

Possible objectives

- To understand the concepts of 'same' and 'different'.
- The understanding of one, two and 'lots'.
- To look at other group members to see what they are holding.
- Engagement in a shared musical game.

Guitar version

A pan-da bear in a zoo was won-d'ring what to do 'cos he was
An e-le-phant in a zoo...

all on his own. A-no-ther pan-da bear came who

looked just the same. They made friends, and then there were two!

Five leaves on a tree

CD track 16

Pat Lloyd

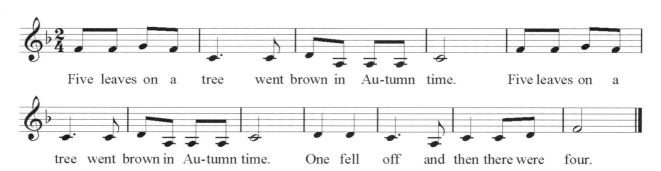

Five leaves on a tree went brown in Au-tumn time. Five leaves on a

tree went brown in Au-tumn time. One fell off and then there were four.

Activities

The focus of the group could be on one branch with five leaves. These could be real leaves or artificial, perhaps made of laminated card on a velcro board. At 'one fell off' a student takes one away. The song ends 'and then there were none'.

The song is best with no accompaniment.

Possible objectives

- Number concepts: 'one' or 'one to five' as appropriate to the individual.

- Linking song with events in nature.

- Anticipating a sequence of actions linked with a song.

Reach out

CD track 17

Activities

An instrument (for example a gong or cymbal) is used as the point of shared focus of the group. For a student with PMLD it may be best to hold the instrument right next to him or her from the start of the song, to give plenty of time in which to respond. For others it may be appropriate to play the sound in the centre of the group and then get closer to an individual as it approaches his or her turn to play.

For those who wish to just feel the instrument, the words can be adapted (e.g. 'Harry feeling this').

Possible objectives

- To touch an instrument and experience the vibratory qualities of the sound.

- To anticipate the approach of an instrument by listening out/looking/feeling.

- To explore sound-making, by reaching out and tapping/sliding/scraping etc.

Guitar version

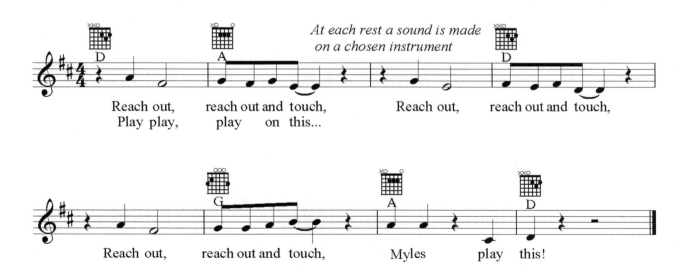

Lorna play!

CD track 18

Pat Lloyd

Activities

This is another song which aims to comment upon students' sound-making, using any instrument or vocalisations. Silent actions such as head-shaking may also provide the central focus of a verse, with the adult taking the opportunity to imitate such actions.

A pause at the end of each verse may allow the student to initiate the next sound/action.

Possible objectives

- To promote explorations of sound-making, using any instrument.

- To allow opportunities for the student to initiate and lead interactions.

- To provide opportunities for the student to recognise imitation of their sounds/actions.

Guitar version

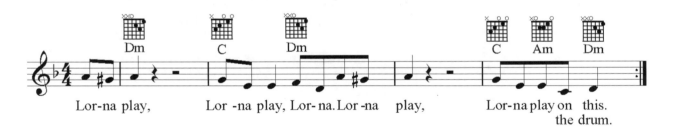

Lor-na play,   Lor -na play, Lor- na. Lor -na   play,   Lor-na play on this.
    the drum.

Let's see what Lorna can do

CD track 19

Pat Lloyd

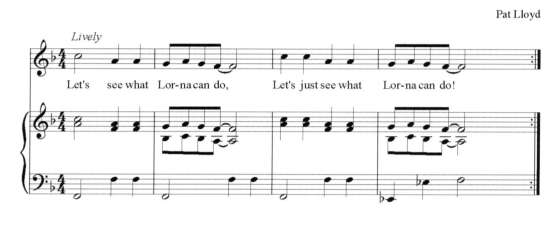

Activities

The song is designed to comment upon a student's actions or sound-making. It would be best if used very flexibly, with long pauses if necessary to allow the student opportunities to lead the play. Imitation of actions/sounds may lead to turn-taking interactions.

An instrument could be used for sound-making, or alternatively purely vocal sounds and actions could provide the focus.

Possible objectives

- The students' recognition of their sounds and actions being copied.

- Opportunities to move or vocalise in response to music and to experience leading the direction of play.

- To experience reciprocal turn-taking.

Guitar version

Playing on the tambourine

CD track 20

Pat Lloyd

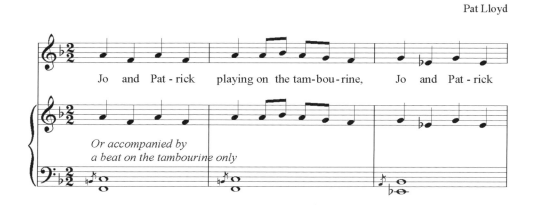

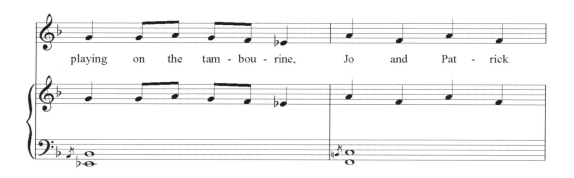

Activities

There are three main ways in which this may be used.

1. One member of staff plays the piano or keyboard, to provide musical support while a second person works individually with each student one at a time. The tambourine is held in between the student and the second person, who share it in their sound-making.

2. The song is sung without piano accompaniment and a shared tambourine is used with the adult providing a beat.

3. Two students could each have a tambourine to make sounds together.

Possible objectives

*   Sound-making with another person in co-active play.

*   Playing with a pulse which then leads the song.

*   Joining in sound-making, following a given pulse.

Guitar version

Hello!

CD track 21

Pat Lloyd

See page 82 for details of activities.

Hello! (2)
CD track 22

Pat Lloyd

He-llo,   he-llo,

he-llo Ha-nnah wel-come!   He-llo,   he-llo,   he-llo Ha-nnah wel-come!

See page 82 for details of activities.

Let's say hello

CD track 23

Pat Lloyd

See page 82 for details of activities.

Goodbye

CD track 24

Pat Lloyd

See page 82 for details of activities.

Activities

These are intended to 'frame' each session with songs which become familiar and associated with the beginning and end of sessions. Due to the value of familiarity it would be best to use the same song each week with an individual or group. The aim is to help students to understand and anticipate what is about to happen, and so for some students this may mean that objects of reference or symbols may also be useful. Some are directed at individuals in the group and are designed to allow plenty of time in which students with PMLD may respond (e.g. 'Let's say hello') and others are songs which are shared by the whole group (e.g. the suggested first verse of 'Goodbye').

Possible objectives

- To recognise and respond to a familiar tune.

- To associate a tune with a particular meaning and to anticipate what is happening next.

- To draw the attention of students to each member of the group.

Guitar versions

For the first 'Hello!' song, the chords are written on the piano version.

HELLO! (2)

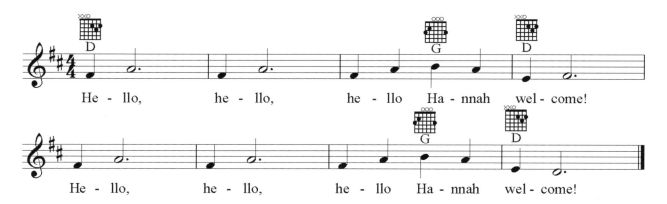

82

LET'S SAY HELLO

Let's say he-llo to An - drew, Oh let's all li-sten to An-drew's sounds

An - drew,   An - drew,   An - drew we're   list-ening to you.

GOODBYE

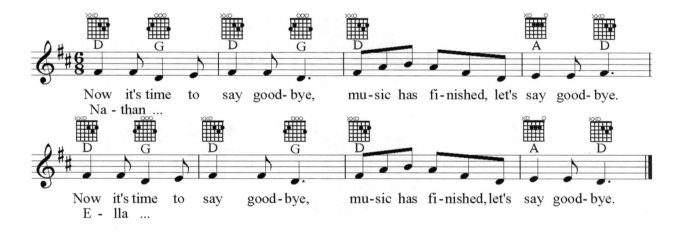

Now it's time to say good-bye,   mu-sic has fi-nished, let's say good-bye.
Na - than ...

Now it's time to say good-bye,   mu-sic has fi-nished, let's say good-bye.
E - lla ...

Shakers do this

CD track 25

Pat Lloyd

Shak-ers do this, shak-ers do this, shak - ers do this just like me!

See page 87 for details of activities.

Adelaide's got bells

CD track 26

Pat Lloyd

See page 87 for details of activities.

Hannah play the drum

CD track 27

Pat Lloyd

Activities

These three songs allow opportunities for sound-making alongside one or more other people. The words should be adapted to comment on the students' actions or sounds (e.g. 'playing quietly, just like Sam'). Support staff could encourage students through imitation, possibly leading to turn-taking. Any responses to the music may lead to opportunities to draw a student into interactions. The use of expectant pauses in between or within verses can be a powerful way of promoting involvement and initiations.

Students could have opportunities for making choices of instruments. The songs may be used individually, or with two students playing together, or as whole-group activities. However, if a whole group of students are making sounds together, it can be most productive to use instruments of the same kind (e.g. all shakers or all bells).

Possible objectives

- To make sounds with others.

- To have experiences of hearing one's own sounds in relation to those of others.

- To draw the attention of the group to its individual members.

Guitar versions

SHAKERS DO THIS

Shak-ers do this, shak-ers do this, shak-ers do this just like me!

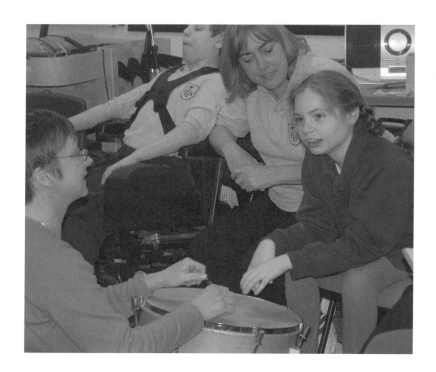

ADELAIDE'S GOT BELLS

A - de-laide's got bells in her hand, A - de-laide's got bells
Jo - na- thon's wav-ing them in the air,

in her hand, A- de-laide's got bells in her hand, Shake, shake, shake!

HANNAH PLAY THE DRUM

For 'Hannah play the drum' the chord of Am could be used rhythmically throughout.

Fireworks

CD track 28

Pat Lloyd

Single switches or Soundbeam are used
to create the sounds of different fireworks

Activities

Soundbeam is ideal for this activity using switches and sensors, and with an appropriate setting for the required sounds of fireworks. Alternatively, acoustic instruments may be used to represent these sounds.

A student or member of staff may provide the drum beat. A member of staff leads the song, each phrase being repeated in call/response style.

Students all have a switch, sensor or instrument with which to make a burst of sound, each playing a solo at the end of each refrain.

At the end all the sounds could be put together.

Alternative words are:
Fireworks at Diwali time…
Time for Diwali, Festival of Light.

Possible objectives

- Vocalising in imitation.

- Making sounds on cue.

- To understand that the sound effects represent fireworks.

- For students to generalise their use of switches.

Going up, going down

CD track 29

Pat Lloyd

Activities

Any of the following 'props' would be useful in adding a shared visual focus to this game: lycra sheet, Rehaband or lycra loop. It needs to be big enough for the group to share by all holding on while standing in a circle. To begin, the lycra (or other prop) is held in mid-position (hip-height), and is gradually raised during the song until the group is stretching up as high as possible at the word 'top'. It returns at the word 'down', with a pause built in to heighten anticipation.

Similarly the lycra is held in mid-position again prior to going down, followed by another opportunity for pausing before returning up.

Once the students know this simple game, they may initiate choice-making, by using gesture or speech to indicate their preference of either 'up' or 'down'. Also the exaggerated use of pauses may allow opportunities for a student to 'fill in' the anticipated word or sound.

Possible objectives

- Sharing a focus of attention within a group activity.

- The simultaneous use of sounds with actions.

- To develop the students' musical understanding of pitch (up/down; high/low).

- To encourage the use of vocal sounds, highlighting exaggerated pitch changes.

Alternative version

If a piano is not available, this song also works well unaccompanied.

Dancing round and round

CD track 30

Spanish folk tune,
adapted by Pat Lloyd

We're danc-ing round and

round, we're danc-ing round in a cir-cle, We're danc-ing round and round, we're

danc-ing round in a cir-cle. We're ...stop! Ja - mie is
and then... Let's co-py

94

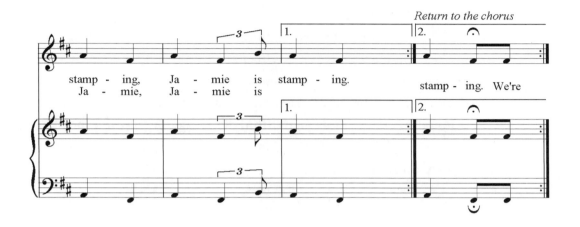

Return to the chorus

stamp - ing, Ja - mie is stamp - ing.

Ja - mie, Ja - mie is stamp - ing. We're

Activities

Students are asked to stand up in a circle and to hold hands, moving round with the song. If holding hands causes too much anxiety, then a Rehaband or lycra loop could be used for students to hold on to. For students who are wheelchair users, the words could be changed to 'We're holding on to the band, and sitting round in a circle'. The experience of moving with a beat can still be created by staff bouncing the band gently, in time with the music.

After the chorus the movement stops, and the focus is on any individual student who is initiating a new movement. (Initially it may be best if a member of staff is ready to model this part of the song, as a means of demonstrating it without a dependency on spoken language.)

Possible objectives

- To have experience of moving with music.

- To anticipate within a repeated play sequence.

- To look at others and to imitate their actions.

- To initiate within shared play.

- To recognise imitation of oneself within shared play.

Guitar version

We're danc-ing round and round, we're danc-ing round in a

cir - cle, We're danc-ing round and round, we're danc-ing round in a

and then...

"Let's look at...
Jamie!"

Return to the chorus

cir- cle. We're ...stop!

Ja - mie is stamp-ing, Ja - mie is stamp-ing
Let's co-py Ja-mie, Ja - mie is stamp-ing.

Holding hands and swaying

CD track 31

Pat Lloyd

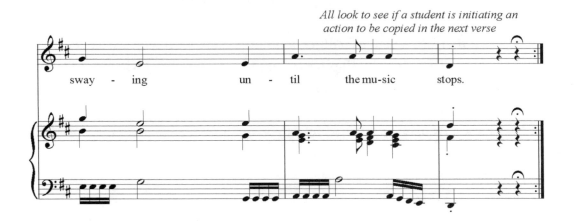

All look to see if a student is initiating an action to be copied in the next verse

sway - ing   un - til   the mu-sic   stops.

Activities

Students sit in chairs in a circle. The music is played/sung slowly with a gentle lilt, and the students are encouraged to sway with the beat. It may help if everyone holds onto a band (e.g. a Rehaband). At the end of each verse, the music stops and there is an opportunity for choosing the next verse, based on the initiative of any of the students.

If there are suitable facilities and staffing, students who are wheelchair users may prefer to sit on mats with physical support. For students with PMLD it may well be best for a member of staff to hold their hands/arms.

The words may be adapted to reflect any appropriate action. For example:
We're clapping hands and swaying...
We're tapping legs and swaying...

Possible objectives

- To experience moving with music and swaying with a beat.

- To gain a shared group focus, in an activity in which all group members have an active role.

- To initiate actions.

- To imitate others' actions.

- To recognise imitation of one's own actions by others.

Guitar version

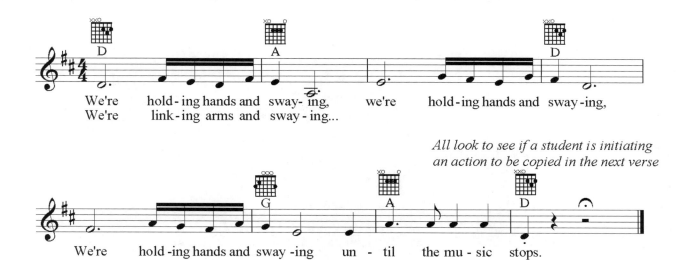

We're hold-ing hands and sway-ing, we're hold-ing hands and sway-ing,
We're link-ing arms and sway-ing...

All look to see if a student is initiating
an action to be copied in the next verse

We're hold-ing hands and sway-ing un - til the mu - sic stops.

Copy me!

CD track 32

Pat Lloyd

a sound is made for the student to copy.

Co-py me, co-py me   Play the mu-sic co-py me

Li-sten Tom, you can be   ve - ry good at   co-pying me!

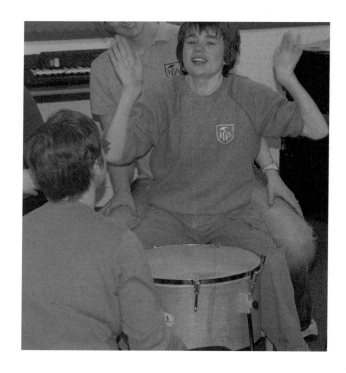

Activities

In each bar's rest, a sound or pattern is made for the student to copy. This could be a hit or scratch on the drum, a rhythmic pattern, or a two- or three-note sequence using pitched percussion. This can easily be differentiated to suit a wide range of needs in the group.

Roles could also be reversed, so that the student takes the leading part.

This is best played without an accompaniment.

Possible objectives

- To imitate one sound when contrasted with a lot of sounds.

- To differentiate between a scratching and hitting sound and to imitate.

- To imitate a pattern of one to three sounds (on pitched or non-pitched percussion).

- To wait for a cue.

Blues in action

CD track 33

Pat Lloyd

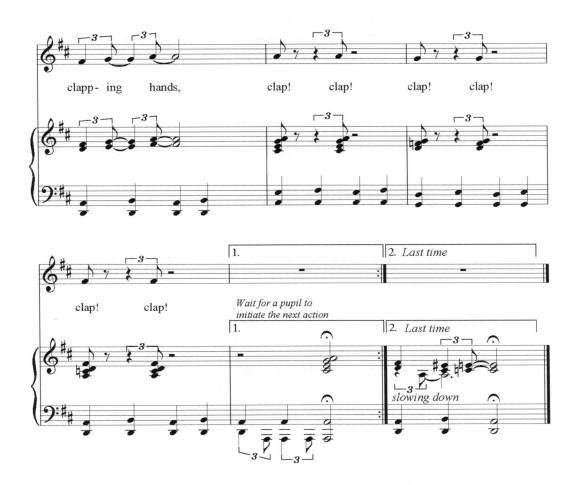

clapp- ing hands,　clap!　clap!　clap!　clap!

clap!　clap!

Wait for a pupil to
initiate the next action

Activities

An action is chosen for others to copy with the song. A support worker could model this to start with. At the end of each verse all look to see if a student is initiating a new action. An unintentional movement may be used for a student who finds it hard to initiate – by others' imitation of the movement, an opportunity has been gained for them to learn that being 'in charge' can be fun!

If a student produces a sound rather than action, this sound could be used instead of words.

Possible objectives

- To gain shared attention within a group.
- For a student to recognise the imitation of his or her own sound or movement.
- To look at the involvement of others and to imitate actions/sounds.
- To take turns as one of a group.

Guitar version

Clapp-ing hands, clapp-ing hands, let's co-py Mi-chael clapp-ing hands,

Clapp-ing hands, clapp-ing hands let's co-py Mi-chael clapping hands,

Wait for a pupil to initiate the next action

clap! clap! clap! clap! clap! clap!

Susie puppet

CD track 34

East European folk melody

Su - sie pupp - et danc - es on your hand she danc - es, Su-sie pupp-et
arm...
leg...

danc - es on your hand she danc - es Mi - chael's
arm... Myles'
leg... Ha - nnah's

No repeat for verse 1 then a
repeat for each additional child

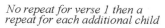

first and last verses

hand hand hand, hand, Su - sie pu -ppet danc - es.
arm arm arm,
leg leg leg,

Activities

A puppet on strings or some types of hand puppet would work for this song. At first the puppet 'dances' for one student, then for the next verse she moves to their neighbour to 'dance', and at the end of the verse she returns to the previous student. It builds up cumulatively, with each subsequent verse adding another member of the group, until all are included.

Students may choose where they would like her to dance, but then need to learn to remember their choice for each of her return visits!

Possible objectives

- To learn to anticipate within the game.

- To experience imaginary play using a puppet.

- To learn to link a song with a sequence of events.

Jumping up

CD track 35

Pat Lloyd

Jump- ing up and saying he-llo to Na-than, jump- ing up and saying he-llo to

Na - than, Jump - ing up and saying he - llo to

pausing to build up anticipation

Na - than... now he's go - ing down!

Activities

This song was written to be used with a pop-up puppet. These are available in many different forms, including puppets of people as well as animals. Each member of the group has a turn at watching with anticipation of the puppet jumping up. A member of staff pops up the puppet on the word 'up' during the song, making the puppet 'hide' at the end of each phrase, ready for the next jump. At the end of the song the puppet stays there for the student to watch, until it slowly goes down at the end.

Pauses can be used throughout to heighten anticipation, and these can be timed around the student's responses.

Possible objectives

- To support the students' understanding of pitch by giving a visual representation of a leap up, in the pitch of a note.

- To encourage students' interest in symbolic representation, using song in conjunction with a puppet.

- To anticipate a strong musical cue in the song, that is heightened by linking it with a visual cue.

- At a very simple level to begin to introduce students to the experience of music being linked to actions and telling a story.

Guitar version

Jump-ing up and saying he-llo to Na-than, jump-ing up and saying he-llo to Na-than, Jump-ing up and saying he-llo to Na-than... now he's go-ing down!

Row boat

CD track 36

Pat Lloyd

*repeat if necessary then
return to the chorus*

hands,　　look　at　your　part-ner,　　find　their　hands.

Activities

There are various possibilities with this song.

1. Students could sit in pairs opposite each other. They may be encouraged to hold hands and to rock backwards and forwards with the music. In the verse section they are to find their partner's arms/shoulders/head, etc.

2. In a mixed ability group that includes students with PMLD, support staff could sit on the floor in front of or behind each student (depending on their needs). The student with PMLD could have the opportunity of experiencing movement with the lilt of the music, with support. In the verse section, their arms/shoulders could be held by the support worker. (Such activities would be best for the student if their support comes from someone who knows them very well. Their expressions of engagement and of preferences may therefore be understood and respected most effectively.)

3. In a mixed ability group that includes more able students, they may be encouraged to sing both parts of the tune. When they are secure in their singing, they could try singing one line on top of the other; they could work towards singing it as a 'round'.

Possible objectives

- To have experience of moving with the pulse of the music.

- To focus on another person and to find their arms/shoulders, etc.

- For students with PMLD to have opportunities to share their responses to the music, and for these to lead to interactions with a familiar adult.

- For more able students to have the opportunity of part-singing.

Guitar version

Row,   row,   row boat   row-ing.   Row,   row,   row boat

row-ing.   row-ing.   Look   at   your   part-ner,   find   their

repeat if necessary then return to the chorus

hands,   look   at   your   part-ner,   find   their   hands.

Let's all make the drum talk

CD track 37

Pat Lloyd

Activities

This is a song in which students take turns at playing a solo. However, during the refrain there could be an active shared role for everyone to play, which could be to tap the beat on their laps or on a small drum or tambour. During each solo passage the accompaniment is repeated but adapted to reflect the student's playing. He or she may choose to continue playing the beat or may wish to explore rhythmic patterns, which the piano or guitar may copy to encourage a dialogue in which the student takes the leading role.

Possible objectives

- To understand the difference between a solo and group playing, and to join in appropriately with each section.

- To take the lead with recognition that their playing affects that of the teacher.

- To engage in a musical dialogue, in which there is reciprocal turn-taking.

Guitar version

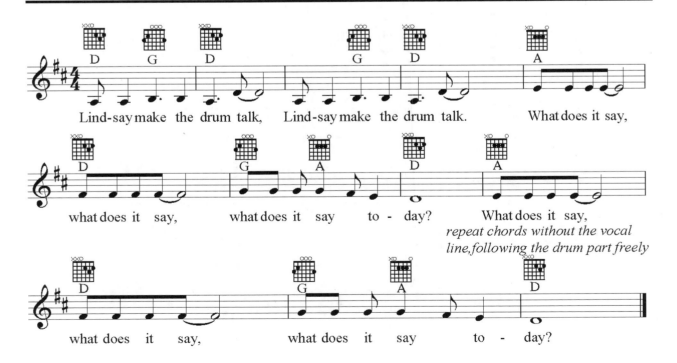

117

Bounce

CD track 38

Pat Lloyd

Activities

The song is designed to be used with a Rehaband, or a broad elastic band made of lycra or rubber, that is big enough to be shared by the group. Support staff encourage the students to hold onto the band, and then the band is bounced gently up and down, in time with the beat. In this way the band and the music provide a shared focus of the activity, and the experience of moving with music, with others.

Alternative verses could include 'Rock…rock with the music, rock, rock, rocking with the beat…' (rocking from side to side).

Possible objectives

- To provide an experience of movement with music.

- To give additional tactile and visual support for understanding that there is a shared focus, by using the band.

Guitar version

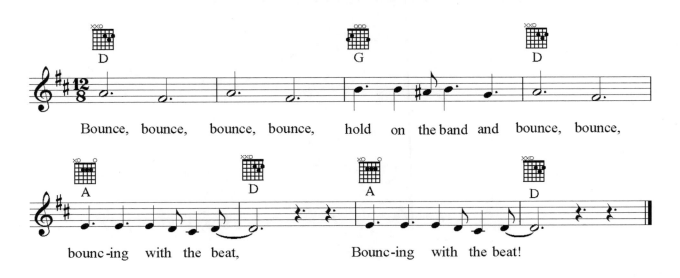

Windy weather

CD track 39

English sea shanty,
adapted by Pat Lloyd

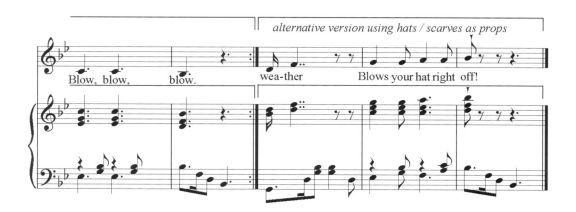

Activities

A member of staff moves between members of the group using a fan to make a 'breeze'. A large Chinese fan is ideal, and very effective at re-creating the experience and sensation of a breeze.

Version 1: Each student in turn experiences the effect of the fan. Nearby staff watch for their responses, which may then lead to interactions between staff and the student. Any initiatives from a student (for example, sound-making or smiling) may be encouraged through adult attention and imitation.

Version 2: As above, but with one or more students wearing a hat or scarf (ideally chosen by each individual). At the end of the song the 'wind' blows the hat or scarf off one student's head.

Possible objectives

- To express responses to a shared physical sensation.

- To express personal preference over whether to wear a hat, and which one to choose.

- To experience hearing a song that describes the sensation that is felt.

Guitar version

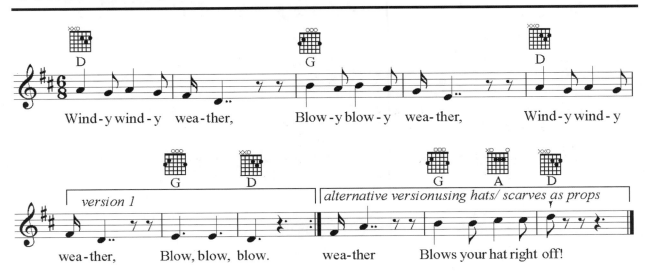

Wind-y wind-y wea-ther,   Blow-y blow-y wea-ther,   Wind-y wind-y

version 1   *alternative version using hats/ scarves as props*

wea-ther,   Blow, blow, blow.   wea-ther   Blows your hat right off!

Follow the leader

CD track 40

Pat Lloyd

At the end of each verse all watch out for a student who may be initiating a sound or action.
He or she then takes the role of 'leader' for others to copy.

Activities

This call/response song can be adapted to suit a range of groups. Students who are able to take turns in vocalising could initially be encouraged to sing Part 2, imitating the short phrases sung by a member of staff who sings Part 1. Eventually students may be able to lead with others providing the imitating role. Alternatively staff could sing both parts, providing a model in which students are supported in any participation.

At the end of each refrain, one student is encouraged to suggest an action or sound for others to copy. The first four bars of the piano part can be repeated several times accompanying the actions or sounds of the student.

Possible objectives

- To take part in a turn-taking game.

- To initiate a sound or action, showing awareness of others' imitation of this.

- To watch and listen to others in the group and to imitate their sounds and actions.

Guitar version

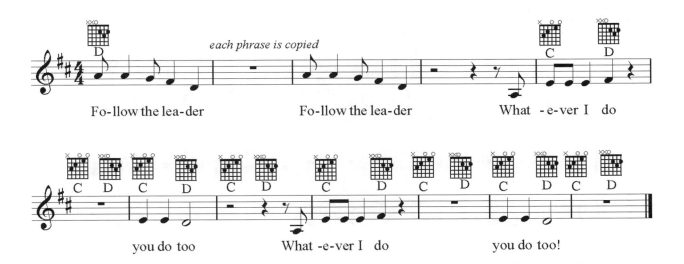

Fo-llow the lea-der   Fo-llow the lea-der   What - e-ver I do

you do too   What -e-ver I do   you do too!

One student does an action or makes
sounds for others to copy.

Hiding game

CD track 41

Traditional Greek singing game,
adapted by Pat Lloyd

Activities

This is a circle game in which the students take turns to find a hidden object. The object could be anything that the students find attractive; this version uses a koosh ball. There could be all sorts of ways of structuring the hiding part of the game, and the words may be adapted accordingly. The following are just two suggestions.

1. The group sit on chairs in a circle. Five identical plastic cups are inverted onto a flat surface – ideally a small table on wheels. One student 'hides' the koosh ball under a cup, out of sight of the others. Another student then searches for the koosh ball, looking under each cup until it is found. This student then 'hides' for the next turn.

2. Three or four draw-string purses are threaded onto a thin lycra loop, which is big enough to be held by all members of the group. One student puts the koosh ball inside one of the purses, and as the music is sung the purses are pushed around the loop, with the help of support staff. Students are then asked 'who can find it?' Whoever finds it then hides it again for the next turn.

Possible objectives

- Attention being drawn to a shared goal within the group.

- Maintaining an interest in a shared activity, even when each student needs to wait for their turn.

- Experiencing the links between music and events, when a song describes the actions within a game.

Guitar version

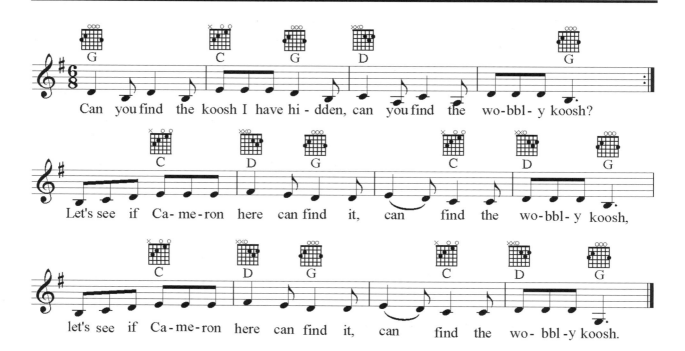

Can you find the koosh I have hi-dden, can you find the wo-bbl-y koosh?

Let's see if Ca-me-ron here can find it, can find the wo-bbl-y koosh,

let's see if Ca-me-ron here can find it, can find the wo-bbl-y koosh.

Play it slowly

CD track 42

Pat Lloyd

Activities

Students will need to have a turn each at this activity. The song has two contrasting sections, and is designed to give students experience of playing with the song, alongside another instrument using slow and then fast speeds. Each section includes an instrumental section, which can be extended as necessary. A sense of anticipation at the end of the slow section can be highlighted by the use of an exaggerated pause.

It may help students' understanding to also use symbols or signs for 'slow' and 'fast'.

Possible objectives

- To recognise the difference between fast and slow.
- To respond differently to contrasting speeds.
- To imitate slow and fast playing.
- To anticipate the point of change within the song.

Guitar version

Play it slow-ly, Ja-mie go slow, take it ea-sy, off you go!

pausing in anticipation

Play-ing fast now, off you go, show us just how fast

Student plays, with guitar repeating the last 4 bars as required

you can go!

Sad and happy

CD track 43

From the spiritual 'Let my people go',
adapted by Pat Lloyd

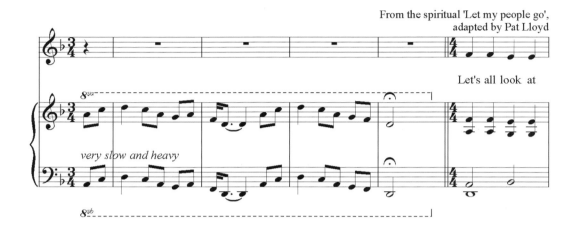

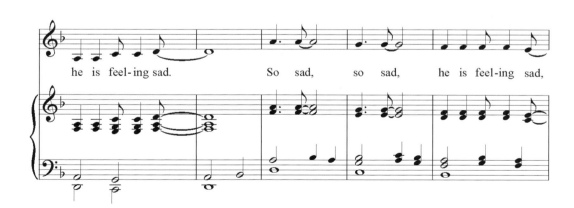

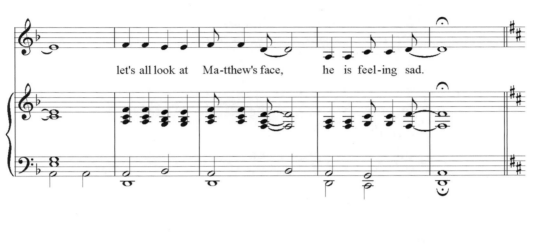

let's all look at Ma-tthew's face, he is feel-ing sad.

Lively and energetic

Chlo - e's feel - ing ha- ppy,

look at her ha-ppy face, she has got a smile! she has got a smile!

Activities

Music is used here to describe contrasting moods. Students with ASD may have difficulties in recognising and understanding emotion, and music, which can communicate emotions so directly, can be used to support such learning. It would be useful to have enlarged symbols and also photographs of faces which express the two emotions. Individual photographs of the students would be ideal, but there are also commercially produced resources on mood recognition that may be useful. The song can be introduced using such photographs for each of the two sections. The accompaniment can be used to exaggerate the differences between the two moods.

A mirror could also be useful, so that, for example, attention can be drawn to the face of a student who appears to be particularly happy.

Possible objectives

- Responding differently to exaggerated musical changes between the expressions of contrasting moods.

- To look at symbols and/or photographs of faces and to recognise happy and sad faces.

- To look at the faces of others in the group and to recognise any particular responses or expressions of sadness/happiness.

Guitar version

very slow and heavy

Let's all look at   Ma-tthew's face,   he is feel-ing sad.   So sad,

so sad,   he is feel-ing sad,   let's all look at   Ma-tthew's face,

he   is feel-ing sad.   *lively and energetic*   Chlo-e's feel - ing

ha - ppy,   look   at her ha - ppy face,   she has got   a smile!

Rocking

CD track 44

Pat Lloyd

With a slow and gentle lilt

quietly

To the left to the right we're rock-ing rock-ing, to the left to the

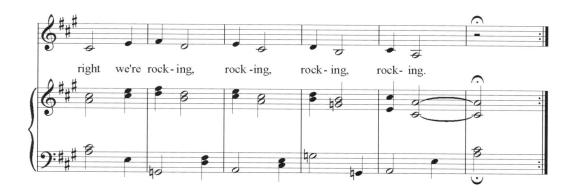

right we're rock-ing, rock-ing, rock-ing, rock-ing.

Activities

There are various possibilities with this song.

1. In a mixed ability group that includes students with PMLD, support staff could sit on the floor behind each student (depending on their needs). The student with PMLD could have the opportunity of rocking with the lilt of the music, with the support of someone who knows him or her well.

2. Alternatively, everyone could sit in chairs in a circle, holding onto a shared lycra band, or Rehaband. Everyone then rocks from side to side with the lilt of the music.

Possible objectives

- To have experience of moving with the pulse of the music.

- For students with PMLD to have opportunities to share their responses to the music, and for these to lead to interactions with a familiar adult.

Guitar version

Let's hear everyone!

CD track 45

Pat Lloyd

Let's hear Clare   playing on the beat now   let's hear Clare   playing on the beat.

Student plays with piano following, repeating ad lib

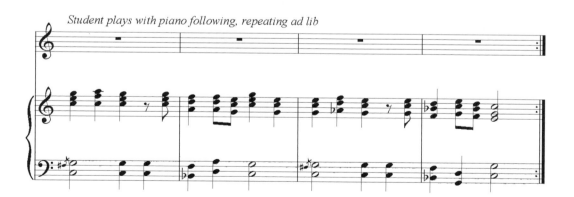

Activities

The song is designed for students who would benefit from support in the development of their sense of pulse. Initially this would be best as an activity in which each student has a solo in turn, with the pulse adapted around the student's preferred speed. After the refrain there is an instrumental section which can be adapted to suit each individual's playing.

As the students progress over time, the words could be changed to accommodate two students per verse (for example, 'Jack and Dulith playing on the beat now' ending with everyone, i.e. 'Let's hear everyone playing on the beat now').

Possible objectives

- To play with a regular pulse and continue when others join in.

- To adapt to a given beat, actively sharing their music-making with others.

- To maintain attention within a group activity, even when not actively having a turn.

Guitar version

Let's hear Clare   playing on the beat now   let's hear Clare

playing on the beat.

My family

CD track 46

Pat Lloyd

Activities

This song was written to support the class theme of 'families'. Some students were very clear about who was in their family, and their relationship to them ('my Mum', 'my brother', etc.), and took great pleasure in singing about them. However, it was much more challenging to recognise and name, for example, their relationship to their Mum (i.e. that their Mum has a daughter/son).

Laminated individual family photographs and symbols with velcro would be useful for many students, allowing them to express their understanding of concepts without a dependency on spoken language. These could be shown on a velcro board, for each student to consider in turn, using the song to add a shared focus and a framework for the activity.

Possible objectives

- For students to share their understanding of their immediate family with their peers and school staff.

- For students to link photographs with general concepts, for example to link a photograph of their Mum with a symbol of 'Mum'.

- To begin to understand others' relationships to them, as well as their relationship to others.

- To learn that other students have family groups of their own.

Guitar version

My fa-mi-ly my fa-mi-ly, Who is in my fa-mi-ly? There's

Mum-my there's Mum-my, Mum-my's got a daugh-ter, that's me! There's

Mum-my there's Mum-my, Mum-my's got a daugh-ter, that's me!

Suppliers and contacts

Chromaharp/autoharp, bass chime bars, puppets and Boomwhackers: Music Education Supplies Ltd, 101 Banstead Road South, Sutton, Surrey SM2 5LH.

Cimbale (simple stringed instrument) and chromaharp: Knock on Wood, Unit 131, Glasshouses Mill, Harrogate HG3 5QH; www.knockonwood.co.uk.

Lycra fabric suppliers: Spentex BCA Ltd, Unit 125, Thorp Arch Estate, Wetherby, West Yorkshire LS23 7BJ; www.spentex.co.uk.

'Rehaband' (designed for use in resistance exercises): Nottingham Rehab Supplies, Victoria Business Park, Pintail Close, Netherfield, Nottingham NG4 2PE; www.nrs-uk.co.uk.

Soundbeam: Soundbeam Project, Unit 3, Highbury Villas, St Michaels Hill, Bristol BS2 8BY; www.soundbeam.co.uk.

WWS and Boardmaker symbols: Widgit Software, 124 Cambridge Science Park, Milton Road, Cambridge CB4 0ZS; www.widgit.com.

CD tracks

1. Let's all listen
2. School song
3. Who is next taking turns?
4. Where is Chloe?
5. Going out!
6. Listen!
7. Five big elephants
8. Taking turns with me
9. Taking turns (for two students)
10. Let's all find each other's shoulders
11. One monkey jumps up!
12. Make him jump up and down!
13. Whose sound?
14. What do you eat?
15. Two by two
16. Five leaves on a tree
17. Reach out
18. Lorna play!
19. Let's see what Lorna can do
20. Playing on the tambourine
21. Hello!
22. Hello! (2)
23. Let's say hello
24. Goodbye
25. Shakers do this
26. Adelaide's got bells
27. Hannah play the drum
28. Fireworks
29. Going up, going down
30. Dancing round and round
31. Holding hands and swaying
32. Copy me!
33. Blues in action
34. Susie puppet
35. Jumping up
36. Row boat
37. Let's all make the drum talk
38. Bounce
39. Windy weather
40. Follow the leader
41. Hiding game
42. Play it slowly
43. Sad and happy
44. Rocking
45. Let's hear everyone
46. My family

Backing tracks (piano only):
47. One monkey jumps up!
48. Make him jump up and down!
49. Adelaide's got bells
50. Blues in action
51. Row boat
52. Rocking